Why Ask ...

Because in Love Sh** Happens!

JUST ABOUT

EVERY QUESTION

TO ASK YOUR *MATE* OR *DATE*

AUTHOR
Indy V. Smith

ART BY
TeLisa Daughtry

ISBN: 978-1-4834-4901-2 (sc)
ISBN: 978-1-4834-4900-5 (e)

Library of Congress Control Number: 2016904675

Cover design © 2015 by YOUniqueverse for Indy V. Smith.

Lulu Publishing Services rev. date: 7/25/2016

Table of Contents

Let's Be Clear

When I took responsibility and began to work on my personal issues, my relationships took on the shapes of normalcy and peace. We all have flaws (including me), but the key is to acknowledge and own them. Over the years, I've had to accept that loving myself means loving all of me and that level of commitment and self-awareness is what we should strive to attract in a relationship. We must be loved for the sum of who we are - not a percentage. Not everyone is going to get you and you're not going to get everyone. Last time I checked, there are a lot of people in this world. We should all be able to get what we need from another person who wants to take the time to understand us.

Why Ask Questions

One of life's most beautiful privileges is the ability to ask a question.

Questions are very powerful. In spite of the fact that as children we were often told not to ask questions, they can be one of the most powerful ways to learn. Examining this discrepancy is one of the best ways to learn. Why don't we feel free to ask more questions - especially when it comes to our relationships? For most people, asking questions can be very intimidating. It's easy to assume they know all they need to know, and it's safer not to run the risk of experiencing any form of hurt or rejection with regards to the answers. In the end, however, people often end up looking foolish and being hurt anyway, simply because they haven't asked the proper questions. When you ask a question, you are asking for someone's inner thoughts; it's a way into the mind of that man or woman with whom you want to grow closer. Questions invite answers, and answers are the key to understanding someone's intellect more deeply. They are a way of uncovering someone's intentions, as well as getting a better perspective of their future vision. When you ask someone the right question, it shows you've taken the time to figure him or her out. That you are asking for an answer proves you are interested and available to listen to his or her wants, needs, and desires. If we fear asking questions, we show that we really and truly are not interested in living in a truthful relationship. If you are not willing to hear what the other person wants and desires, what's the point of getting to know that person? If you are afraid of getting an honest answer about what it is they have to offer, what relationship longevity can you expect to have? Some people are in such a rush to get the loving feeling of connection. They miss the joy of developing that connection. Why rush anything you want to spend so much time enjoying? Really and truly, relationships start with you and your honesty. They start when you ask the right questions of your self-first: Who am I? What do I truly need and want? Before the questions begin, I'd just like to explain the premise behind this book. This concept came from my honest desire to ask questions as a child. I've always had a desire to understand why things are the way they are. Why this? Why that? Why not? How come? I've always had a natural desire to ask questions and now that I'm an adult with adult perspectives I see the importance of an issue magnified. This book was designed for those who need help trying to figure out the right questions to ask their desired partner or to see if they are with the right person to begin with. It is also designed to help you reach into yourself and find your questions before making severe and significant commitment choices. For starters, make a commitment to yourself! Promise that you will ask questions about everything you want to know about yourself, your partner and your relationship. And be prepared to answer just as many questions as you are asking. Let's get started!

Communication & Needs

If you don't understand your needs, how can you expect anyone else to know what they are

Communication is essential, but what are you communicating? People say that before you get into a relationship with someone else you need to have a relationship with yourself but what does that mean? Who are you? What are you going to communicate to someone else if you don't know who you are? How can you expect to build a relationship if you can't even answer this question? I think communication falls apart when we're not clear about our needs. Understanding our needs is just as important in a relationship as ~~air is to~~ breathing air is to life. Now let's be clear: we also have desires. However, our desires are different from our needs. Needs must be met however desires one may go without having them fulfilled. I think it's important to know yourself and understand your needs with clarity in order to clearly communicate them to others.

Here are some great questions to enhance your communication skills:

- What are some negative barriers that might affect your relationship?
- After an argument do you need time to cool off or do you need to come to a resolution immediately?
- Do you embrace communication?
- What are some things that you tell yourself that may or may not be true, especially those things the other person in the relationship should know about?
- What part did you play in the breakdown and misunderstanding in your last relationship?

- What did you learn from your previous relationship that will help in your new relationship?

- What are some changes that need to be made in your life that can help enhance our relationship?

- What are some of your relationship expectations?

- Are you open to counseling?

- How do you feel about relationship titles, Do you mind if we have titles early on in the relationship?

- With regards to your emotions, how important is it to have the support of your significant other?

Once again, your needs are paramount. Without understanding our selves and needs it's going to be very difficult to communicate anything to anyone else. We cannot expect another person to fulfill those needs if we don't understand them first. Think about it like this: if you're hungry, you need to feed yourself. It's the same with communication, emotions and relationships. These things must be fed.

Ask Indy

To Thine Own Self Be True

"Hi Indy my name is Dee, and I'm not sure what I want. Indy, I have been living with my boyfriend for six months now, and it is the hardest experience ever. He is a great guy, but he acts as if we are married. He has so many rules for me like I have to call when I'm out late. Some of my male friends he's not happy with and the clothes that he use to like to see me in he now says are too revealing for work. I'm not sure if he's trying to control me or protect me. Help! Is this the man for me or is this a disaster waiting to happen?"

My dear Dee,

Let me say this: some individuals are better at hiding their personality and behavior abnormalities. Romantic relationships can be beautiful with the right person. A relationship with the wrong person, however, can lead to years of heartache, emotional damage, and even physical harm. We must learn from our mistakes and change ourselves accordingly to be whom we want to be, however when someone is actively trying to change who you are this is not a good sign. The changes that need to be made need to be made by you first not forced by another person. When you love someone you can't help but want to give them everything – right? If your boyfriend is unwilling to see the damage he is doing with regards to his delivery, then that may be more of an issue than what he is complaining about. The fact of the matter is you need to understand your personal needs. What is it that is important to you? What do you need

to be a happy, emotionally stable and a physically healthy person? You'll need to determine if the relationship is taking something away, and, if so, put an end to the destructive cycle.

In my opinion Dee it sounds as though you have your answer, merely from asking the question.

— *Indy*

Your Personal Questions

Trust

Trust You First

If you learn to trust yourself then you will learn that others should earn your trust. You need to understand trust and that if you don't have it in your relationship then your relationship has nothing to stand on. Without trust, people are uncomfortable every day all day, and that's just the truth. If you don't trust the person you are with then you shouldn't be with them.

Here are some realistic questions: These are important questions to ask, especially if your partner tries to intimidate you when you do or refuse to give you an answer:

- How important is trust for you in a relationship?

- What are your views on monogamy?

- Is cheating a deal-breaker?

- What do you consider cheating?

- Do you feel comfortable expressing yourself or your insecurities when they come up?

- Are you constantly on social media?

- Are they're any persons in your life that could affect our relationship in a negative way? If so, are you willing to remove them from your life?

- Do you have a need for excessive female attention?

- Do you have a need for excessive male attention?

- Are you comfortable establishing and honoring barriers in order to protect our relationship?

- Do you need your significant other to post your relationship on social media?

- Do you need privacy with regards to your cell phone or would you mind sharing the password?

- If we are not formally committed with rings or engagement, do we have the option to date openly while in this relationship?

These are just some questions to think about and consider when discussing the area of trust. We need to be real about who we trust, how we trust, and how we define trust. These hardcore questions can lend a hand in this area of your future or present relationship. I suggest you write down your own question; these are just a few to get you through the initial steps of trust.

.

Your Personal Questions

_____
_____
_____
_____
_____
_____
_____
_____
_____
_____
_____
_____
_____
_____
_____
_____
_____
_____
_____
_____
_____
_____
_____
_____
_____
_____

Emotions

Our thoughts lead us to act on our feelings.
Clear Thoughts Aid in clear emotions.

Okay so let's be emphatically honest and clear: the emotional stuff that we need to discuss is going to be embarrassing and challenging at first, but it must be done. Sensitive topics are going to come up anyway seeing as though we are human and carry our feelings everywhere on our life's journey. If you don't bring up the hard stuff, the emotionally charged realities in the beginning when you are getting to know one another trust me, it is going to play out later. Your relationship expectations will not be met. So let's get to the mushy emotional stuff in the beginning. Even if the relationship turns out differently from what was expected, at the very least the initial groundwork was laid with transparency, good intentions - and the right questions.

- Can you say with clarity and truth that what you say you want from a relationship today will be what you want in the future from a relationship?

- Do you think you are in a place in your life when you are ready to share your life and are you interested in being a part of another person's life?

- Do you want to be a part of my life?

- Can you see me as a complimentary and positive life partner for you? Please explain?

- What does it mean to you to take care of your significant other?

- How do you envision being taken care of emotionally, mentally, and physically?

- What are some of your insecurities if any that may affect our relationship?

- What do you want from a woman?

- What do you want from a man?

- Are you looking for a relationship to fill a gap, a whole or space in your life?

- Are you at peace and comfortable being in a monogamous relationship right now and what does that look like to you?

These are just some of the emotional questions that can be asked and brought up. Emotional questions are meaningful, however, if we don't get the answer we want, it can lead to feelings of rejection. But it's better to ask them and know then not to ask and assume the answers.

Your Personal Questions

Sex

Sex starts in the mind, so be clear about how you prefer to be pleased.

- What sexual activities do you enjoy the most?
- Are there specific sexual acts that make you uncomfortable? Be specific!
- Do you enjoy receiving and giving oral sex?
- Do you enjoy role-play?
- Do you have any sexual fantasies?
- Do you feel comfortable initiating sex?
- If yes, please explain? If no, please explain?
- Do you need to be in the mood for sex?
- Have you ever been exposed to or know anyone who was exposed to any sexual abuse or sexual assault? (This is a tough and personal topic and should be handled with care)
- How were you taught about sex as an adolescent?
- Was sex talked about openly in your home?
- Who taught you about sex?
- If something upsets you, do you use sex for comfort?
- Is sexual fidelity an absolute necessity?
- Do you enjoy viewing pornography?
- How often do you need or expect sex?
- Have you ever had a sexual relationship with a person of the same sex?

- Has sexual dissatisfaction ever been a factor for you in the breakup of a relationship?

- Have you ever had a threesome?

- Do you need to have one if you haven't already?

- Have you ever had group sex?

- Do you desire to have group sex if you haven't already?

- How often do you watch porn?

- Do you need porn to perform sexually?

- If you do watch porn, do you like to watch it alone or with your significant other?

- Do you enjoy including toys in your sex life?

Ask Indy

Not On The Same Sex Page

"Dear Indy, My girlfriend wants to have sex daily and I do not. What to do? I know this sounds silly, but my girlfriend wants sex every day and I do not always feel like having sex. I just don't. Sometimes I wish to express intimacy without sex. But as much as we discuss it, and as much as she says she "understands," she still presses for sex and when she doesn't get it says she feels "rejected." I try to explain that if we have sex Friday and Saturday, but I don't feel like it on Sunday, then you aren't being rejected, but she won't listen. In fact, every time I try to express how I feel about it, she starts to cry which I am beginning to suspect is a subtle form of manipulation to get me to cave in. I don't know what to do. She is the love of my life, but I can't keep having the same argument every two weeks for the rest of my life."

Ok, Mr. Sex Toy

The bottom line is you should be able to reject **her** offer to have sex without her exploding, and that is as much on you as it is she. If she does feel so rejected anytime you are not in the mood for **sex** that it makes her cry, then I think therapy is needed. The two of you could seek help as a couple and find out what the real issue may be with her. This is to **say** her sexual + emotional needs are important, and **so** are yours, and one should not automatically take precedence over the other. Once she has the fear of rejection issue addressed, you guys need to come to an agreement about how you both can get your needs met that can be a win-win.

— Indy

Your Personal Questions

_____
_____
_____
_____
_____
_____
_____
_____
_____
_____
_____
_____
_____
_____
_____
_____
_____
_____
_____
_____
_____
_____
_____
_____
_____
_____

Appearances

Is Image Everything? Keep It Right Keep It Tight?

According to Psychology Today, we all know that looks matter. What most of us don't understand is just how much looks matter, and how difficult it is for us to ignore a person's appearance when making a social judgment. I'm not talking just about romantic relationships; I'm talking about all of our human interactions. And by appearance, I'm not speaking directly of the *"beauty"* dimension, but also of many other qualities of one's appearance (Mlodinow 2012).

In reading some other professional opinions, I came across this perspective on appearances: "I think that attraction that is not physical can end up being physical eventually when you grow to care about someone. Listen, I'm not going to lie and say that personal grooming and cleanliness aren't important, they obviously are. But at the end of the day, you need to be with someone who wants you for whom you are and respects how you want to present yourself. Not someone who wants you to look like they want you to. How you choose to present yourself does say something about you, we can't pretend it doesn't. But one of the most powerful things it can say is that you care enough to take care of yourself." (Wiest 2013).

- How important is it that you always look your best?
- How important is your partner's appearance?
- Do you have strong preferences about being with a particular physical type?
- Are there cosmetic procedures that you regularly undergo?

- Are you opposed to plastic surgery?

- Is weight important to you?

- What would your reaction be if your partner were to gain a significant amount of weight?

- How much money do you spend on clothing at any given time?

- Do you worry about aging?

- Do you worry about losing your looks?

- What do you like and dislike about your appearance?

- When you were a child, were you often complimented or shamed about your looks?

- What would your reaction be if your spouse lost a limb or any other body function?

- What would your reaction be if your partner lost a breast to cancer?

- How would you handle hair loss?

- Do you feel that you can have good chemistry with someone who you find to be moderately physically attractive?

- How much is strong physical attraction necessary?

Your Personal Questions

_____
_____
_____
_____
_____
_____
_____
_____
_____
_____
_____
_____
_____
_____
_____
_____
_____
_____
_____
_____
_____
_____
_____
_____

Day-to-Day Commonalities

What we do today will determine our tomorrow.

Commonalities can be the shared values, interests and create the essential identity between two people. The more things a couple have in common the more likely they are to have a solid friendship base which are the most important characteristic of a healthy relationship. A solid friendship base is imperative to a prosperous relationship. Sometimes chemistry can develop in later stages, but it cannot survive without friendship. Sooner or later we get out of bed and have to build a life together. The more we share, the easier it is to grow. However, friendship is the glue that keeps us together.

- Do you enjoy traveling?
- How often would you like to travel?
- Where would you like to travel?
- How important is it to you to spend time alone?
- How would you feel about me going on a trip with the girls/boys for a couple of weeks?
- How important is spending time with friends to you?
- What would we do if we both had a break from work, but each of us had different ideas on how to spend it?
- Would you consider yourself a morning person or a night person?
- Are you a physically affectionate person?
- Do you mind public displays of affection?
- When you have a disagreement, do you tend to debate or withdraw?
- Do you consider yourself an easygoing person?

- How much sleep do you need a night?

- What is your idea of relaxing?

- What makes you furious?

- How do you and how have you reacted when you're infuriated?

- What makes you most insecure?

- How do you handle your insecurities?

- What makes you most secure?

- Do you fight fair? Ask for examples.

- How do you celebrate when something great happens?

- How do you mourn when something tragic happens?

- What are some of your social limitations?

- What are some of your best strengths?

- What does a dream marriage look like to you?

- What are some of your fears?

- What drains you of your joy and passion?

- What feeds your mind, body, and spirit?

- What makes you smile in tough times?

- What makes you feel the most alive? Are you an animal lover? Do you have a pet?

- Do you think if you love me, you will love my pet?

- Have you ever been physically aggressive with an animal?

- Have you deliberately hurt an animal?

- Do you believe a person should give up his or her pet if it interferes with the relationship?

- Do you consider pets members of your family?

- Have you ever been jealous of a partner's relationship with a pet?

Ask Indy

Can The Need For Sleep Ruin The Intimacy In A Relationship?

"Dear Indy, I need some advice. As I type this letter, my husband is sleeping, and I am wide-awake and full of energy. The last two days I came home from work late afternoon, and he went to bed for a nap. When he is up and full of life, I'm falling asleep on the couch or already in bed..... I'm a night person, and he is a morning person. I never thought this would or could affect our marriage, but it is. I want my husband to stay up with me and do things. I wish I had given this more thought before we married ten years ago. I caution others to contemplate this heavily.

Please Help! Nancy"

Nancy, I know this will sound a bit harsh, but it is my truthful opinion that this isn't as bad as you perceive it. The bottom line: people are different. Work with what you have, but try working with your fantasy too. Sometimes a little change of perspective makes one enjoy a wider variety of life's pleasures. I think that you just have to accept your husband the way he is. People are who they are. Just enjoy what time you have with him. It's entirely possible for things to work between a couple, who are on different schedules if you both are willing to compromise with one another's schedules.

— Indy

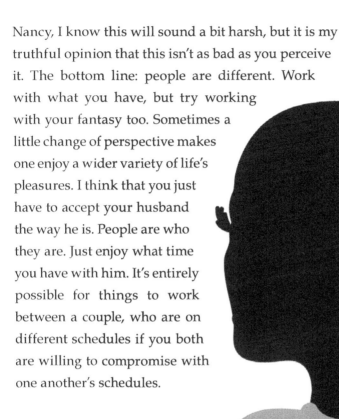

Your Personal Questions

_____
_____
_____
_____
_____
_____
_____
_____
_____
_____
_____
_____
_____
_____
_____
_____
_____
_____
_____
_____
_____
_____
_____
_____
_____

Birthdays & Holidays

Love is a celebration; a date just makes the memory memorable

- Are holidays important to you?

- Do you like to celebrate holidays?

- Do you consider birthdays special?

- How do you celebrate birthdays?

- Should a couple spend all holidays and birthdays together?

- Do you like to exchange Christmas presents?

- Do you like to receive and give birthday presents?

- What was the most romantic gift you gave to a significant other for their birthday? How was it received?

- What was the most romantic present you gave to a significant other for Christmas? How was it received?

- Do you think there should be a budget for purchasing presents?

- Do you enjoy surprises when receiving gifts or do you prefer to know ahead of time so that you receive what you desire?

- Would you return a gift you didn't like? Would you let your significant another know if it weren't to your liking?

- How long into the relationship would you want to be in before giving and receiving presents?

Ask Indy

Who is really on your VIP list?

"Dear Indy, My boyfriend, does not think it is important that I am at his birthday party or that we spend holidays together. He firmly believes that there is no need to spend the holidays away from your family. I am struggling with this because, I think when you are in a committed relationship, living together and in love, you should spend the holidays together, perhaps alternating whose family you spend the holidays with. Am I expecting too much, or should I cut my losses?

Samantha, BK, NY"

Clearly you're uncomfortable with these developments because you wrote in, so it sounds like while he might be a great guy, this isn't the best relationship for you. You don't have to break up with him this minute, but you do need to adjust your expectations about where your relationship is headed and start being open to meeting someone else and ultimately moving on.

You need to decide if it's important to you. And if it's important to you, then you need to make it clear to your boyfriend that it's important to you. If your boyfriend doesn't care about things that are important to you, then there is something wrong with your relationship, I don't care how many good qualities he has. Sometimes in relationships, you need to communicate very clearly what you need.

— Indy

Ask Indy

Is it me or do you just detest Santa?

"Hi there. I need some advice. I love the holidays; it's just a spirited time of year, and I'm a lively person. I love the positivity in the air. Last year I had only been with my boyfriend for six months so I didn't ask him to celebrate Christmas with me, and I spent it with my family. I noticed he didn't give me a card or anything. I thought maybe it was because the relationship was new. This year I asked him if he would please celebrate it with me. I have explained to him several times that holidays are important to me, and that I really would appreciate it if he would make some kind of effort. I've only received a card from him and never any gifts. But back to asking for Christmas. He said no and flat out refused to spend it with me. I explained it could be simple, low key and that he could make me a card/homemade gift. He doesn't have a job, and I understand that. He said that he flat out refuses because "he doesn't want to, and he doesn't care about the holidays."

Why does he refuse? I know in his last relationship he celebrated Christmas with his ex every year and all holidays she got gifts. He says it is because she made him. I don't want to make him. But I don't understand why he won't do for me what he did for another woman? I just want a loving card and for him to not be a Grinch all month. I want to make Christmas cookies and just enjoy the spirit. I just feel bummed because I know he has celebrated it before but won't even compromise halfway for me. I don't even know how to bring it up again without him getting mad.

Please Help!"

It seems your issue is less about Christmas and more about respect and compromise. A healthy relationship affirms who each person is and allows each person to meet his or her needs together. A conflicting relationship demands that one or both partners change in an in-depth way to meet the needs of the other person, which compromises one or both of the persons involved. This is unhealthy compromise. In the case of Christmas I can see where he could be a bit more amenable but if he doesn't want to be willingly you shouldn't give up something that you love because he isn't showing an interest. You shouldn't compromise your joy. Too often it can happen that we give in and agree to compromises because we think it will save a troubled relationship. It sounds like you may be trying to save something you are uncertain about. Sometimes when we are faced with losing someone that we are desperate to keep in an unhealthy way, we compromise to keep the relationship together, the compromising should stop.

— *Indy*

Your Personal Questions

Health

If we have our health, we have everything.

A deeper level of commitment will arise when health issues come into play. It's easy to be committed to your relationship when it's going well, but when someone gets ill that can be a real test of faith, love and patience. Health issues can be a relationship changer, however, shouldn't we expect real challenges? Some sacrifices need to take place for the relationship to grow and move forward.

- How would you describe your current state of mental, emotional and physical health?

- Have you ever had a severe illness?

- Have you ever had surgery?

- Are they're any genetic diseases in your family or a history of cancer, heart disease, or chronic illness?

- Do you have health insurance?

- Are you big on physical fitness?

- How much time do you spend at the gym every week?

- Have you ever suffered from any disorders?

- Have you ever been in a serious accident?

- Do you take medication?

- Have you ever needed to take any medication?

- Have you ever had a sexually transmitted disease?

- Have you ever been treated for a mental disorder?

- Do you see a therapist?

- Have you ever had a need to speak with a therapist?

- Do you smoke, or have you ever smoked?

- Is smoking a deal breaker?

- Would you consider yourself having an addictive personality?

- Have you ever suffered from an addiction?

- Have you ever been told you have an addiction problem, even though you might disagree?

- How much alcohol do you drink at any given time?

- Do you use recreational drugs?

- Are recreational drugs a deal breaker?

- Do you have a medical problem that may impact your ability to have a gratifying sex life?

- Examples: erectile dysfunction, premature ejaculation, vaginal dryness, and drug or alcohol addiction.

Your Personal Questions

_____
_____
_____
_____
_____
_____
_____
_____
_____
_____
_____
_____
_____
_____
_____
_____
_____
_____
_____
_____
_____
_____
_____

Children & Parenting

Just because someone can reproduce, doesn't mean they should. Parenting isn't for all of us.

- Some people aren't parent material but can be an excellent babysitter. Which one are you?

- Do you want children? When? How many? Are you able to have children?

- Would you feel unfulfilled if you were unable to have children?

- Are you on birth control?

- What would you do if there were an accidental pregnancy before you planned to have children?

- What is your view of fertility treatments? Adoption? Would you adopt if you were unable to have a child naturally?

- What is your view on abortion? Should a male partner have an equal say in whether his wife/girlfriend has an abortion? Have you ever had an abortion? Has a past lover ever had an abortion?

- How important is it to you that your children are raised near your extended family?

- Do you believe in spanking a child? What type of discipline do you believe in practicing?

- Do you believe that children should be raised with some religious or spiritual foundation?

- In a blended family; should birth parents be in charge of making decisions for their children?

- Would you ever consider getting a vasectomy or having your tubes tied? Do you believe it's your choice, or does your partner have a say?

Ask Indy

A Want To Be Dad

"Dear Indy, I'm 33 and my wife is 32. We've been married for five years and have a pretty good life—a nice house, interesting jobs, a great group of friends. Of course, our relationship isn't perfect (whose is?). But I never had serious doubts about our future until recently, when my wife made it clear that she does not want to have children. She has always been ambivalent about kids. Why did I marry her you wonder? When we met, we were so young that I figured her views would change as we gained the financial means to support a family. While I would never force her to have children if she doesn't want, I also don't know if I can be happy forfeiting my chance to be a father. I love my wife and don't want to leave her. But I'm still relatively young.

Should I get out while I still have time to start over?"

My sense is that you have had many indications along the way that your wife would not ultimately want to have children. Presumably, you have been with her since she was in her late twenties. You state that you figured she would change. Instead, fantasy has now set reality, which eventually happens when the assumption is that the other person in the relationship will do the changing.

It is important for you to acknowledge that your wife has a clear vision on her decision not to have children. You must accept that she is not going to "give in" and that you cannot change her mind. That leaves only one decision, and it is yours to make: Do you stay in your marriage and forego fatherhood, or do you leave the relationship to pursue a new path with the hope and expectation that it involves fatherhood?

First of all, consider what it is about fatherhood that appeals to you. Are there ways to accomplish that without having children of your own? For example, if you have nieces and nephews that live close by, you could strive to be the most involved uncle in the world from infancy on up. Or you could volunteer in a mentoring program for children.

In other words, there may be lots of ways to enjoy children, and to provide them with love that may be satisfying to you.

— *Indy*

Your Personal Questions

Extended Family & Friends

Sometimes your friends & family can be the enemy of your relationship

- Are you close to your family?

- Do you have a difficult time setting limits/boundaries with your family?

- Have you identified the childhood wound that may have sabotaged your relationships in the past?

- How important is it that you and your partner are on good terms with each other's families?

- How did your parents settle conflicts when you were a child?

- Do people in your family carry long-term grudges?

- How much influence do your parents still have over your decisions?

- Have unresolved or ongoing family issues ever been a factor for you in the breakup of a relationship?

- Do you see a close friend or friends at least once a week?

- Do you speak to any of your friends on the phone everyday?

- Do you believe in having friends of the opposite sex?

- Do you have clear boundaries with your friends regarding your partner?

- Do you prioritize your relationship in a manner that your friendships don't compromise your relationship?

- Are your friendships as important to you as your life partner is?

- If your friends need you, are you there for them?

- Is it important to you for your partner to accept and like your friends?

- Is it important that you and your partner have friends in common?

- Do you have a difficult time setting limits with friends?

- Has a partner ever been the cause of breaking up a friendship?

- Have friends ever been a factor for you in the breakup of a relationship?

Your Personal Questions

Relationship History

The best predictor of our future outcomes can be hidden in our past choices.

- Have you ever felt insecure about a relationship? How did you get over the insecurity?

- When was the first time you felt that you were in love with another person?

- What happened in that relationship?

- What is the longest relationship you have ever had?

- Why did it end, and what lesson did you learn?

- Have you ever been married?

- What was the reason for the divorce?

- What part did you play in the breakup?

- How did you handle the breakup?

- Do you have children from a previous marriages or non-marital marriage? What is your relationship like with them? How would you prioritize our relationship and your previous one?

- Have you ever been engaged to be married but the wedding never happened? Why didn't the wedding take place?

- Have you ever had a live-in partner?

- Why did you choose to live together instead of marrying? What did your experience teach you about the importance of marriage and commitment?

- Do you harbor fears that the person you love might reject you or fall out of love with you?

Your Personal Questions

_____
_____
_____
_____
_____
_____
_____
_____
_____
_____
_____
_____
_____
_____
_____
_____
_____
_____
_____
_____
_____
_____
_____
_____
_____
_____
_____
_____
_____

Career & Goals

Both parties in the relationship should have ambition.

- Are you working in your chosen field?

- How many hours a week do you work?

- What does your job entail? (For example, do you often travel for business, work at home, perform dangerous tasks?)

- What is your dream job?

- Have you ever been called a workaholic?

- What is your retirement plan? What do you plan to do when you stop working?

- Have you ever been fired?

- Have you ever quit a job suddenly?

- Have you changed jobs a lot?

- Do you consider your work a career or just a job?

- Has your work ever been a factor in the breakup of a relationship?

Your Personal Questions

Finances

Money can't buy you love, but it can be rented from time to time.

Stress over finances can devastate a relationship. The effects of financial distress can include blame, panic and lack of intimacy. In some cases, unresolved financial issues can lead to a breakup or even a divorce if you are married. It is important for a couple to work together to resolve issues that bring about financial stress. A relationship takes two partners to work. Both people must be dedicated to being open and honest while dealing.

- Do you believe that a certain amount of money should be set aside for pleasure, even if you are on a tight budget?

- Have you ever used money as a way of controlling a relationship?

- Has anyone ever tried to control you with money?

- Has money ever been a factor for you in the breakup of a relationship?

- How important is it for you to make a lot of money?

- Do you or have you ever created any past relationship debt? Do you pay alimony or child support?

- Do you believe in prenuptial agreements?

- Do you believe in a budget?

- Should individuals within a marriage have separate bank accounts in addition to joint accounts?

- Do you feel that bills should be divided based on a percentage of each person's salary?

- Who do you believe should handle the finances in the relationship?

- Do you have a significant amount of debt?

- Do you gamble?

- Have you ever been called cheap or stingy?

Ask Indy

Is Masculinity Defined By Finance

"My name is Adam I'm 40, and a successful accountant at a small firm. My wife, a doctor, still earns more than me. At first, I was embarrassed by my wife's breadwinner status. "It was a male ego thing," "There was just something about it that made me feel inadequate". I knew it was illogical.

Three years ago, after nearly six years of marriage, my resentment bubbled over when my brother asked why we never had children. "I made a rude comment about how my wife was too busy wearing the pants in our relationship to be a mom", "And then instantly regretted it."

I feel really bad, but I'm not sure how to handle my feelings, I don't want to disrespect my wife, I love her and appreciate her support."

Adam, I need for you to go to your wife immediately and apologize. Ask what you can do to be more supportive and express and discuss the salary differences and the toll it has taken on your self-esteem. For the first time, you will show your true feelings and work them out together. It won't be the money that will affect your relationship it will be the lack of communication. There are so many more important things to worry about in life than who makes more money.

— *Indy*

Your Personal Questions

_____
_____
_____
_____
_____
_____
_____
_____
_____
_____
_____
_____
_____
_____
_____
_____
_____
_____
_____
_____
_____
_____
_____
_____
_____
_____
_____
_____

Your Living Environment

Home Is Where Peace Resides or At Least It Should

According to The Michigan News of University of Michigan overall, three key reasons for living together emerged: wanting to spend more time with one's partner, wanting to share life's financial burdens, and wanting to test compatibility. But the way men and women talked about these three broad reasons was very different. Women volunteered "love" as a reason to live together three times as often as men did while men cited "sex" as a reason to live together four times as often as women did. But what about other living challenges. As far as long distance relationships are risky, and if you are unfortunate enough to be far away from your significant other, the prospect of potentially ruining your relationship can seem daunting. Just because long distance relationships are difficult, doesn't mean they're impossible. Simple adjustments to your attitude and lifestyle can help you keep your loved one in your life. (Swanbrow 2011)

- If you could live anywhere in the world, where would it be?

- Do you prefer urban, suburban, or rural settings?

- Is it important to have your private home, or do you prefer apartment or condo living, with a management company responsible for the maintenance?

- Do you prefer to clean your home or hire a housekeeper?

- Is it important that your home be quiet, or do you prefer having music or some background noise most of the time?

- Is it important to have a TV in the bedroom? Living room? Kitchen? Do you like to sleep with the TV or radio playing in the background?

- How important is it for you to have space in your home that is yours alone?

- Have differences about home style ever been a factor in the breakup of a relationship?

Ask Indy

Should I Stay Or Should I Go?

"I live in Houston, and my boyfriend is looking for a job in Dallas. Since he wants to have a job and be settled before he proposes, we wouldn't be engaged before moving. My problem is that I'm so wary of moving in with a boyfriend (even in the same city) because it may turn out badly because it has turned out badly in the past for me. Not to mention I don't want my friends/family to think I'm just a girl who just follows a guy wherever he goes because I'm needy or something.

I know that I want to be with my pre-fiancé (lol...sounds better than a boyfriend) forever, and he's a great guy who I know will always be there for me no matter what. But when he asked me if I would go with him if he got this job the other day, I hesitated and said "maybe." I don't want to be far from my family (and his as well), but I know that getting this job would be a natural progression for him but will it be grate for our relationship.

Decisions, decisions..."

If you move and the relationship doesn't work out, are you going to resent your partner? If the answer is "yes," that doesn't necessarily mean you shouldn't move, but you should probably spend some good time thinking about the very real possibility that things might not work out. If that risk seems too great for you—if the idea of making such a significant sacrifice without experiencing the payoff you're hoping for and will leave you feeling bitter and regretful—you probably aren't quite ready to make the leap yet.

Have you discussed a long-term future together? It doesn't necessarily have to involve marriage, but if you and your partner aren't considering a long, serious commitment together, uprooting your life and moving to a new city is probably premature. You both need to imagine a life together at least five years in the future and not be freaked out by that idea before you start packing your bags. And if you aren't on the same page as far as your future goes, forget about it!

Is the new city one you can picture yourself being happy living in? You need to accept that love doesn't conquer all. You may love your sweetie something awful, but if you hate the town he lives in, there's a good chance you're going to be miserable there. If you aren't sure how you feel, spend your vacation time—a week or two if you've got it—"playing house" at your significant other's place and trying to imagine how you'd feel if you never left.

— *Indy*

Your Personal Questions

Emotional Intelligence

After spending over fifteen weeks researching and covering Emotional Intelligence, I couldn't imagine writing this without including some basic information on EI. It is important to understand that without the display of emotional-intelligence a relationship is doomed. Both individuals in the relationship have a personal responsibility to developed their awareness and understanding of emotional intelligence. There are five main areas that help to characterize a person's emotional intelligence, which can contribute to alert someone if they are ready for the committed relationship they claim to want.

According Goleman (2004) there are five components of Emotional Intelligence: Self-awareness - The ability to recognize and understand your moods, emotions, and drives, as well as their effects on others.

Self-regulation - The ability to control or redirect disruptive impulses and moods. The propensity to suspend judgment and to think before acting is a critical part of self- regulation.

Motivation - A passion to work for reasons that go beyond money or status. Some may even consider this to be an individual's passion or purpose.

Empathy - The ability to understand the emotional makeup of other people, which requires an understanding of how to react to another person's emotional state.

Social Skill -The ability to develop and manage relationships.

By definition, Emotional Intelligence is not commonly understood or put into action on a consistent basis. According to Goleman, (2004) it would seem as though Self- Awareness would be the first in the five areas of Emotional Intelligence that would be of value to implement in one's day to day activities. As it is a very crucial area of a person's personality, most are not aware of what it means to understand one's self and lack the understanding of one's individual Emotional Intelligence within the area of Self–Awareness itself (Goleman, 2004). I urge everyone to consider how Emotional Intelligence can enhance not only their relationships but for your individual personal growth.

{ Wrapping Up

Finally, it's extremely difficult, if not impossible, to have a loving relationship with another person if you dislike yourself. I don't think there's anything wrong with taking some time off from dating to build a healthy relationship with you for you before building a relationship with someone else. In fact, more people should try it!

The lessons I've learned through dating really great men, bad boys, boring men, and damaged men, through breaking hearts and having my own heart broken are lessons that I wouldn't change at all. This book is a product of my pain and growth as a woman and I hope for it to be a product for your gain on new perspectives on asking the right questions. The greatest lesson I've learned through the years of growth has been honesty. Being and remaining honest with your self is paramount for peace and it promotes gaining respect from the other person. To be clear, questions aren't meant to intentionally offend anyone however they should spark conversation and those who are uncomfortable with the intended truth should be carefully observed while dating. Make the commitment to your safety, commit to your well-being, commit to loving you first.

Hugs and Kisses — *Indy V. Smith*

Acknowledgements

It goes without saying my first acknowledgement goes to the practice of gratitude, without gratitude my connection to the Creator would not be activated. I am truly grateful for my spirit guides and the gifts they bestow upon me. This project is from spirit through me to you.

I would like to show my gratitude to one of my college professor Dr. Richard Grallo for his inspirational perspectives, theories and lectures on the importance of asking question. It was one of his lectures that literally sparked the light that started this book. I must admit my attention was no longer with the lesson of the day however the lesson was affective in me creating the blueprint of Why Ask…

I must also thank more of my college professors who include Dr. Anisia Quinones, Dr. Charles Gray, and Dr. Adel Weiner who all have aided in my growth and current psychological perspectives. To my dear friend Lenny Green, I thank you for my radio platform, which has allowed me the exposure to many listeners who want to discuss their journey through love and relationships. I am truly grateful for my friend Global Vito for supporting me in my radio career and motivating me with regards to taking my life's next major steps.

I cannot and will not forget my Beloved, for which the foundation of my questions came. As our new relationship has grown many of the questions included in this book were asked of you and answered openly and consistently, for that I am grateful. The relationships I am blessed to have in my opinion are of a higher purpose and have supported my growth as a person and an author.

I would like to express my gratitude to my dear friend TeLisa Daughtry who saw me through this book; your creative talents and design ideas are outstanding and have brought this book to life. To Shannon Dohar who provided support, talked things over, read, offered comments, assisted in the editing, and proofreading, I thank you.

Last but not least: To my Mom and Dad the love and support from you both is undeniable. You both have always supported my efforts, which have aided in me becoming the me I am meant to be. And for that I am grateful.

And to you the readers, I thank you for your support with all my projects, for supporting my perspectives. Thank you for trusting my advice and thank you for sharing your experiences with me. It takes true vulnerability and sincerity to show up and discuss your life, for that I am and will always be grateful.

Your Personal Questions

_____
_____
_____
_____
_____
_____
_____
_____
_____
_____
_____
_____
_____
_____
_____
_____
_____
_____
_____
_____
_____
_____
_____
_____
_____
_____
_____
_____

References

Mlodinow, L. (2012, June 11)

How We Are Judged by Our Appearance

Retrieved March 10, 2015

https://www.psychologytoday.com/blog/subliminal/201206/how-we-are-judged-our-appearance

Wiest, B. (2013, March 28)

Physical Appearance Should Not Be The Most Attractive Thing About You

Retrieved March 10, 2015

http://thoughtcatalog.com/brianna-wiest/2013/03/physical-appearance-should-not-be-the-most-attractive-thing-about-you/

Swanbrow, D. (2011, February 11)

He says, she says: Men and women view living together very differently | University of Michigan News

Retrieved March 10, 2015

http://ns.umich.edu/new/releases/8260References

1/21/2021

Call in about when to leave a relationship
— Melinda — when you're not happy

Erica — leave when it no longer serves you

Tips on how to be
happy between
Relationships

Made in the USA
Columbia, SC
18 December 2020